Kids Can Press acknowledges the financial support of the Government of Ontario, through the Ontario Media Development Corporation's Ontario Book Initiative; the Ontario Arts Council; the Canada Council for the Arts; and the Government of Canada, through the BPIDP, for our publishing activity.

Published in Canada by
Kids Can Press Ltd.
29 Birch Avenue
Toronto, ON M4V 1E2

Published in the U.S. by
Kids Can Press Ltd.
2250 Military Road
Tonawanda, NY 14150

www.kidscanpress.com

Edited by Stacey Roderick and Karen Li
Designed by Marie Bartholomew
Printed and bound in China

The hardcover edition of this book is smyth sewn casebound.
The paperback edition of this book is limp sewn with a drawn-on cover.

CM 08 0 9 8 7 6 5 4 3 2 1
CM PA 08 0 9 8 7 6 5 4 3 2 1

Library and Archives Canada Cataloguing in Publication

Hughes, Susan, 1960–
    No girls allowed : tales of daring women dressed as men for love, freedom and adventure / Susan Hughes ; Willow Dawson, illustrator.

Interest age level: Ages 9–12 years.
ISBN 978-1-55453-177-6 (bound). ISBN 978-1-55453-178-3 (pbk.)

1. Male impersonators–Biography–Juvenile literature. 2. Transgender people–Biography–Juvenile literature. 3. Transvestites–Biography–Juvenile literature. I. Dawson, Willow II. Title.

HQ76.97.H84 2008   j306.77'80820922   C2007-906084-6

Kids Can Press is a **Corus** Entertainment company

No Girls Allowed

Tales of Daring Women Dressed as Men for Love, Freedom and Adventure

Written by
Susan Hughes

Illustrated by
Willow Dawson

Kids Can Press

To sweet Fiona, who asked to hear the stories — S.H.

This book is for you, Dad. Thank you for teaching me how to draw,
how to play a saw and, most importantly, that girls are allowed!
Special thanks to my husband, Ray, and to Karen L., Susan, Marie, Karen B.
and the rest of the KCP gang — W.D.

Contents

Hatshepsut

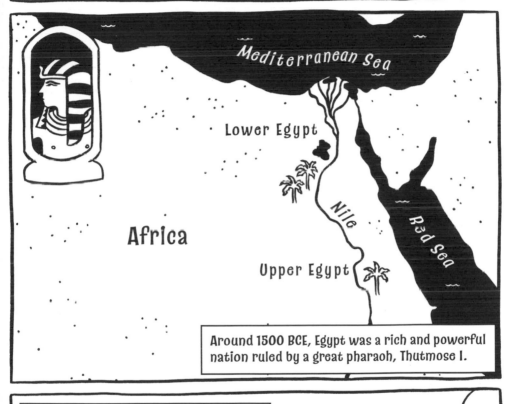

Mediterranean Sea

Lower Egypt

Nile

Red Sea

Africa

Upper Egypt

Around 1500 BCE, Egypt was a rich and powerful nation ruled by a great pharaoh, Thutmose I.

Thutmose I treated his only daughter, Hatshepsut, very well. Unlike other girls of this time, she grew up knowing a lot about politics and power.

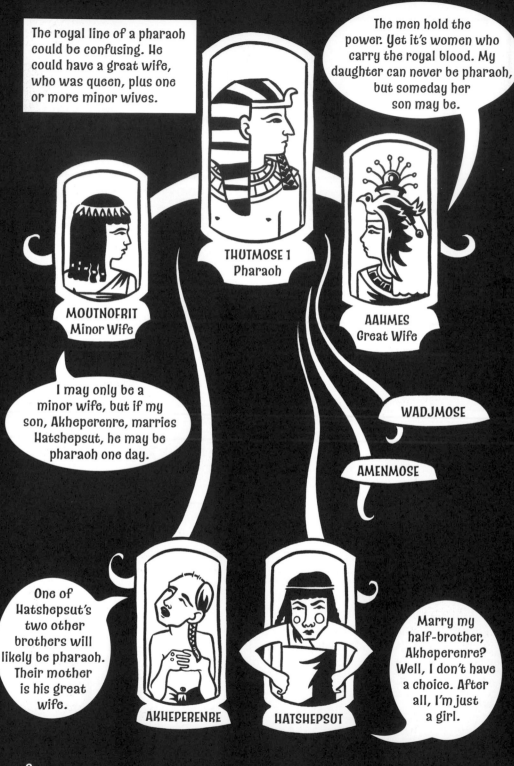

Hatshepsut, the baby's aunt and stepmother, was chosen to be the regent and to rule until Thutmose III was old enough to reign.

But she wanted more ...

11

13

About 15 years after Hatshepsu became pharaoh, her nephew grew old enough to take power. No one knows whether or not Hatshepsu gave up her throne voluntarily.

Around this time, Hatshepsu disappeared. She may have retired or perhaps died. Some even say she was murdered.

Hatshepsu's name was erased from many monuments and replaced with Thutmose III's name.

For centuries, no one knew the unacceptable truth that a woman had once been pharaoh — or where Hatshepsu's remains lay. In 2007, her mummy was finally identified in an unmarked tomb.

Mu Lan

Around 1400 years ago, a poem was written in northern China. It recorded the legendary tale of a brave girl named Mu Lan. Her story continues to be told today.

Look, Mu Lan!

Oh, no. Messengers from the Khan!

The Khan was the powerful Mongolian ruler who governed a vast Asian Empire, including China.

When the Khan needed help fighting the tribes of Northern China, he drafted more soldiers into his army.

The Khan wants one male from each household.

To go to war could mean death for a brother, father or son.

Mu Lan, aren't you going to look?

Why? I have no brothers and my father is too old to fight.

Yes, and your father never lets anyone forget how much he'd prefer a son.

Mu Lan! My father's name is here! Your father's, too!

The Khan cannot expect my father to fight! He wouldn't survive the journey to meet the troops!

I must protect him somehow ...

Mu Lan was happy to remove her armor and live as a woman again. But after some time, she received a letter ...

So my army companions have learned who I really am. They want to come and see me. Do they think I betrayed their trust?

It's true. She's a woman!

I ... I am pleased to greet you again.

Mu Lan, you are remarkable.

A fine daughter and an incredible warrior!

The famous poem does not explain how Mu Lan spent the rest of her days. But it ends with these words about Mu Lan's disguise ...

"Two hares running side by side close to the ground, How can they tell if I am he or she?"

Alfhild

In the 9th century, farmers and fishers lived peacefully in the kingdoms of Scandinavia. But there were also the Vikings, Scandinavian warriors and traders who sailed to other parts of Europe and North America to trade, raid and loot. At this time, there lived a beautiful princess.

Arctic Ocean

Scandinavia

How are you this morning, Alfhild?

Fine, Mother.

Princess Alfhild, daughter of King Siward, was so beautiful that her parents kept her in a cabin, hidden from men.

28

33

Esther Brandeau

But that very night, Esther's ship ran aground ...

40

41

It seems that Esther stayed in New France for about one year, living at a hospital and then in several private homes. She refused to be converted. The law said she had to be shipped back to France and tried at court. On September 27, 1739, Intendant Hocquart wrote to the French Minister ...

At times she was quite dutiful and obedient to the instruction given her by the priests, while at other times she was very obstinate. I cannot do anything but send her back.

No more was heard of this adventurous young woman. It is likely that she left New France. But to where? Perhaps she managed to find another way to freedom ...

48

James Barry

January 1810. The world was changing, but women in many countries, including this one, Scotland, still did not have the same rights as men.

Atlantic Ocean

Great Britain

Mother, I'd like be a doctor when I grow up.

Don't be silly, dear. Girls can't be doctors.

Aunt Mary Anne, I'm home!

Good evening, James.

Three more years of anatomy, surgery, botany, chemistry, theory and practice of medicine ...

Then I'll be the first woman to become a doctor in all of Scotland, maybe in all of England.

Of course, it will have to be my secret.

It's believed that James's real name was Margaret Buckley or Miranda Stuart and that James's "aunt" was really her mother.

One day you will go to the Royal College of Surgeons in Edinburgh.

The best medical school in the world!

But, Mother, with Father in debtor's prison, how can we afford it?

Even if people believed James was a young man, it was expensive to become a doctor. Possibly James was helped by an uncle, James Barry, who was a famous painter.

Africa

The Cape was a British colony overseen by a governor, Lord Charles Somerset.

Ah yes, I've heard of this chap. Bright, opinionated, likes parties. And this letter from Lord Buchan recommends him.

After working for several years in a British military hospital, 25-year-old James arrived in Cape of Good Hope, South Africa. Slavery was legal here. Those with money lived very well, but the needy were often forgotten.

Lord Somerset and James became good friends, spending a lot of time together in between James's many duties.

We'll head out to the leper colony now, driver.

Yes, sir.

In November 1827, the Colonial Office finally admitted James had been unfairly dismissed. She received a promotion to Staff-Surgeon of the Forces.

James left South Africa in 1828. She went on to serve in the Caribbean, in Malta and in Corfu. Everywhere she went, she was known as an outstanding surgeon, an expert in infectious diseases ... and an interesting fellow.

There's that extraordinary doctor.

And his latest dog. Each one of his poodles has been named Psyche.

Pillows ... we'll replace straw with feathers. Mattresses ... we'll replace straw with hair.

In 1857, James was posted to the British Empire's coldest colony, Canada. Within a year, she was promoted to the most senior rank possible, Inspector General of Military Hospitals.

In May 1859, James became ill and returned home to England.

No! I don't wish to be examined!

James died six years later. When she was laid out for burial by the maidservant, her secret was discovered ...

Dr. McKinnon, Dr. Barry's death certificate says he's a man, but he's not. I saw the body myself.

It's none of my business whether Dr. Barry was a man or a woman. He's dead and so I signed the certificate.

James Barry — the talented doctor whose work in so many countries had benefited millions of people — was a woman! The public was amazed. Yet it wasn't until 1876 that Britain allowed women to enter all medical professions.

Ellen Craft

In 1837, slavery was legal in the southern United States. Thousands of people had been kidnapped from Africa, brought to the United States on ships and sold as slaves. Their masters put them to work and treated them poorly.

Mama, I don't want to go!

Honey, you know you have to.

Ellen, an 11-year-old slave, was a wedding gift to the daughter of the family, the newly wed Mrs. Collins, who was leaving home to live with her husband.

United States

The Crafts fled to England in 1850. They worked with anti-slavery organizations for years and finally returned to the United States in 1869, four years after slavery was abolished.

Sarah Rosetta Wakeman

New York State, 1862. Disagreements about power and slavery caused eleven southern "Confederate" states to leave the Federal Government of America, or the "Union." The Confederate states and the Union states were at war.

Nineteen-year-old Sarah Rosetta Wakeman worked hard on her parents' farm, attending school when she could.

In 1864, the regiment was sent to the Red River Campaign in Louisiana. It took 10 days to march to Alexandria.

Here they joined other troops. Maybe Rosetta would have felt less alone if she'd known that hundreds of other disguised women were fighting on both sides of the war — including Jennie Hodgers, known as Albert Cashier.

Private Cashier?

Yes, sir.

On April 9, 1864, Rosetta went to battle on the front lines for the first time.

When will this stop? We've been fighting for hours!

Afterword

Kids hear "no" a lot more than adults do. And, unfortunately, throughout history and in almost every single country, girls and women have heard "no" more than boys and men have. "No, you can't do that." "No, you can't go there." "No, you can't study that." "No, you can't vote."

Women could not vote in Canada until 1917 (and 1940 in Quebec) and until 1920 in the United States. The first medical school for women was not founded in Japan until 1900, and women were not allowed into the American Medical Association until 1915. Women could not get pilot licenses in Canada until 1928. And NASA only started accepting female astronauts in 1977. It was not until 1995 that women could become judges in Iran, and it was only in 2003 that Pakistan began permitting women to train as fighter pilots in their armed forces.

Is it any wonder that so many girls have grown up thinking that their gender limits them?

But not all of them believed it.

This book is about seven women who just wouldn't, or couldn't, take "no" for an answer. They were born and lived within a wide range of historical time periods and cultures. Their tales will take you from 1470 BCE to the mid-1800s, from ancient Egypt to the American Civil War. Each woman was born into a unique set of circumstances and needed to conceal her identity for a different purpose: Hatshepsut wanted power; Alfhild wanted adventure; Margaret Buckley wanted a career; Ellen Craft wanted freedom from slavery.

Bravely, desperately, each woman made the same radical leap for freedom — she would change her name, her appearance, her identity ...

and "become" a man. There would be dire consequences if she were discovered; each considered the risk worth taking.

When disguised as men, they were treated differently by the people in their society. They were allowed to do more, say more, and they were given more respect than they had had as females. And, in each case, although all that they had changed was their clothing, they suddenly felt safer, smarter, more capable and more ambitious. Allowed the freedom to reach out and try, they could achieve their goals. Unfortunately, they had to do it while living a lie.

There are many more equally fascinating stories of women in disguise that just couldn't fit into the pages of this book, and it was great fun to research these "tales of daring women." At the same time, it was disheartening to have so many historical examples to choose from, so many girls who had to resort to subterfuge in order to follow their own path in life.

Today, there are still countries where men and women are not given equal rights and equal opportunities. In some countries, education for girls is considered a frill, not a necessity. Women continue to be more affected than men by religious and societal beliefs. Certain dress or behavior, such as wearing a bikini or simply traveling alone, might be considered "improper." And in times of war or upheaval, women are usually in much more danger than men of having their freedoms taken away.

It was, however, reassuring to find that more recent examples of women disguising themselves as men are harder to come by. More commonly, women are now being promised equal treatment by law, including equal pay, equal opportunities for education and equal rights to vote. In many countries around the world, women can become prime ministers and presidents; they can aspire to the highest levels of education and pursue the career of their choice; and they can earn good incomes and travel freely and independently.

I enjoyed writing about the adventures of these seven remarkable girls and women – and I hope you've enjoyed reading about them! I hope their unpredictable stories of independence and bravery persuade you to believe, as strongly as I do, that appearances can be deceiving. People should never be limited by others' assumptions about them. Everyone deserves an equal chance to reach out and try.

Further Reading

Hatshepsut

Hatshepsut: The Princess Who Grew Up to Be King

Read about Hatshepsut's childhood in Egyptian palaces and her journey to becoming pharaoh. Includes color photographs. Written by Ellen Galford (National Geographic Society, 2005).

Mu Lan

The Song of Mu Lan

A beautiful picture book translation of the Chinese folk poem "The Ballad of Mu Lan." Illustrated by Jeanne M. Lee (Boyds Mills Press, 1991).

Alfhild

Booty: Girl Pirates on the High Seas

A collection of true tales about real women pirates who sailed the high seas. Recommended for young adult readers. Written by Sara Lorimer, illustrated by Susan Synarski (Chronicle Books, 2002).

Esther Brandeau

Esther

A children's novel based on the remarkable adventures of Esther Brandeau. Nominated for the Governor General's Award for Children's Literature. Written by Sharon McKay (Penguin Group, 2004).

James Barry

With a Silent Companion

A children's novel inspired by the extraordinary achievements of Margaret Anne Buckley, otherwise known as James Barry. Written by Florida Ann Town (Red Deer Press, 2004).

Ellen Craft

5,000 Miles to Freedom: Ellen and William Craft's Flight from Slavery

The dramatic true story of Ellen and William Craft. Includes maps and photos. Written by Judith Bloom Fradin and Dennis Brindell Fradin (National Geographic Society, 2006).

Sarah Rosetta Wakeman

An Uncommon Soldier: The Civil War Letters of Sarah Rosetta Wakeman, alias Pvt. Lyons Wakeman, 153rd Regiment, New York State Volunteers, 1862–1864

A collection of Sarah Wakeman's letters. Recommended for young adult readers. Edited by Lauren Cook Burgess (Oxford University Press, 1996).